Awake and Rise

Bite-sized examinations for deepening the deconstruction process

The Path of Unlearning: Book Two

Other Deconstruction Books

Sleeper, Awake: 40 days of companionship for the deconstruction process

Books in the Where True Love Is Devotional Series

Where True Love Is: an affirming devotional for LGBTQI+ individuals and their allies

Transfigured: a 40-day journey through scripture for gender-queer and transgender people

I Don't Want Them to Go to Hell: 50 days of encouragement for friends and families of LGBTQ people

Pro-Life, Pro-Choice, Pro-Love: 44 days of reflection for finding a third way in the abortion debate

A Theology of Desire: Meditations on intimacy, consummation, and the longing of God

Sex With God: Meditations on the sacred nature of sex in a post-purity-culture world

Transgender Relationship Books

Holding On to Hope: Help for friends and family of transgender people

Reaching for Hope: Strategies and support for the partners of transgender people

Novels

The Language of Bodies

Kristy's Story

Children's Books

Jamie the Germ Slayer

Rumplepimple

Rumplepimple Goes to Jail

Awake and Rise

Bite-sized examinations for deepening the deconstruction process

Suzanne DeWitt Hall

The Path of Unlearning: Book Two

Copyright © 2024 by Suzanne DeWitt Hall

All rights reserved. No part of this publication may be reproduced, distributed, or transmitted in any form or by any means, including photocopying, recording, or other electronic or mechanical methods, without the prior written permission of the publisher, except in the case of brief quotations embodied in critical reviews and certain other noncommercial uses permitted by copyright law.

Bible passages included in this book are from the World English Bible unless otherwise indicated.

DH Strategies

First Edition

ISBN-13: 978-1-7347427-9-4

Printed in the United States of America

Dedication

It's been a strange few years for my beloved and I, with many things changing. But one thing remains, and always will:

All my books are for and through you, Declan.

I love you.

Contents

Introduction i
    Divine Pronouns iii
Counting the Cost 1
    Day 1:   Loss of Reliance on Scripture 2
    Day 2:   Loss of Church 3
    Day 3:   Loss of Language 4
    Day 4:   Loss of Relationships 5
    Day 5:   Loss of Certainty 6
    Day 6:   Loss of a Sense of Mission 7
    Day 7:   Loss of Sacraments 8
    Day 8:   Loss of the Holy Family 10
    Day 9:   Loss of identity 11
Things Biblish 13
    Day 10:   The Bible as False Idol 14
    Day 11:   The "Bible Alone" Myth 15
    Day 12:   What Did Jesus Say? 16
    Day 13:   Colonization of Scripture 17
    Day 14:   Experience is Important 18
    Day 15:   Inerrancy and Infallibility 19
    Day 16:   Bible as Parable 21
    Day 17:   Seek Incandescence 23

Things Churchish 25
    Day 18:   Church as False Idol 26
    Day 19:   Clergy as Mini Gods...27
    Day 20:   Whose Words are Whose? 29
    Day 21:   Hotbed for Abuse 31
    Day 22:   Childish Things...33
    Day 23:   Having "Enough Faith" 35
    Day 24:   A "Right Way" to Pray 36
    Day 25:   The Problem of "Mission" 37
    Day 26:   Savior Complex...39
    Day 27:   Colonization of Peoples 40
    Day 28:   Invisible Bars of Control...................................42
How Tos 45
    Day 29:   Pray for Wisdom...46
    Day 30:   Remember Humility...48
    Day 31:   Ask Why You Believe What You Do...................50
    Day 32:   Stop Striving...51
    Day 33:   Resist the Urge to Blame 53
    Day 34:   Listen for the Divine Whisper..........................54
    Day 35:   Reincarnate Here and Now 55
    Day 36:   Ask Questions...56
    Day 37:   Invite Wonder...57
    Day 38:   Resist the Urge to Reinstate Order..................58
    Day 39:   Be Careful with People 59
    Day 40:   Look Toward the Light 61
    Day 41:   Laugh a Little 62
    Day 42:   Increase Your Awareness of God in All Things 63
    Day 43:   Keep Going..65
Conclusion..67

INTRODUCTION

Eclosian: *the act of emerging from the pupal case or hatching from the egg. Caterpillars unforming and reforming into something new.*

If you've already deconstructed to the point of atheism, this book isn't for you. It's written for people who feel a connection to Christianity but find aspects of it problematic and want to examine that discomfort to see if there's a way to co-exist with tenets of its teaching.

Evaluation of the version of Christian faith we've individually been taught is like a maze. You enter eagerly or with trepidation, and once in, are presented with opportunities to choose paths. Sometimes the quest is easy and you quickly find yourself outside in the sunshine and breeze again, ready to move on to your next adventure. Other times the choices seem overwhelming, the towering branches above threatening, and you wander around for a long time, testing, reversing, and growing confused and angry as no completion point seems near.

Regardless of which way your own quest unfolds, try to view your exploration as a spiritual labyrinth rather than a monster-filled maze, in which you seek the center and then continue out again, all the time inviting openness of your spirit, and allowing each step to reveal whatever there is to be revealed in that specific place, at that specific moment. A space for meditation, contemplation, renewal, and reassurance.

Introduction

This book is designed to help you inhabit that space. It's a book to confirm you aren't crazy.

Contemporary Christianity is riddled with problems, but there's still room in all of us for the divine.

Divine Pronouns

As my years of unlearning have unfolded, my language has as well. I've abandoned the idea of a solely male deity and envision instead a divinity who is neither male nor female, while simultaneously both male and female as described in the Genesis creation accounts. Here are the pronouns I use throughout the book when describing the Christian understanding of God as a trinity:

      Creator They/Them/Theirs
      Jesus He/Him/His
      Holy Spirit She/Her/Hers

Counting the Cost

Christianity is not merely a faith tradition, it's also a cultural experience which impacts numerous aspects of our lives. In this section we'll discuss things which are sometimes lost during the deconstruction process and consider how to cope with those losses.

DAY 1: LOSS OF RELIANCE ON SCRIPTURE

If you're deconstructing, your view of Christian scripture has probably shifted and is quite likely to continue to transform. But this is an urging you might not expect:

Try not to throw the Bible away entirely.

Truth can be found in every path which seeks the divine, and sacred writings of every religion contain elements of that truth. So try to accept that while the Bible has been misrepresented and misused by Christians for centuries, it *can* still be a means of accessing insight. Humanity's searches for God have meaning.

To do this you have to relinquish a number of concepts. You'll need to let go of the idea that the Bible is inerrant, divine, and has universal application. You'll have to stop reading literalistically and embrace historical context and human massaging of messaging. Once you do all that—and you've probably done some of it already—you'll need to stop being angry about it.

And then see what happens.

For me, it's meant seeing God's breath as a call to the hungering hearts of the authors as they struggled to make sense of a confusing world. It's meant pondering the power and importance of myth, and the difference between truth and fact. It's meant realizing God could inspire writers to tell stories which teach through negative example rather than outright instruction.

As you continue to crack the chrysalis of your faith, your view of the Bible will keep changing, but that doesn't mean you have to discard it entirely. The vision you hold of it just needs to change with you.

Growth, survival and even salvation may depend on the ability to sacrifice what is fictitious and unauthentic in the construction of one's moral, religious or national identity. One must then enter upon a different creative task of reconstruction and renewal.
Thomas Merton

Day 2: Loss of Church

Over the course of years my spouse and I have left churches due to geographical moves, discriminatory theology, and ugly church splits. Each of these goodbyes hurt, some more devastatingly than others. Since then we've attended services in a variety of places, but are too burned out by bad experiences and too far along in our deconstruction to be more than tourists in any congregation.

The first few months after leaving our last church were intensely uncomfortable, but the time away gave us room to think about Christianity as an institution, about individual congregations, and about what church is and could be.

Church offers community, prayer, discussion about the Bible, the sacraments, and a sense of mission and contribution. Good ones might even be active in the work of social justice. When deconstruction results in cutting ties with those things, the losses can have a profound impact on your life.

On the plus side, severing the cord can also mean disconnecting from immutable politics, freeing up money and time, and gaining the mental bandwidth to evaluate your past years of experience.

As you process your emotion, remember that leaving church doesn't mean losing God. In the end, you may discover you're able to encounter God more deeply. But it *will* be different.

> *Jesus of Nazareth was not a Christian. This should be obvious and self-evident. There is a real question as to whether he intended us to become "Christians" after he was gone. In my view, the answer is just as obvious. No. Jesus did not come to found a new religion. On the contrary, his life and message was essentially the announcement that the time for religion had ended, and that what people had hoped to find through religion they could find inside themselves.*
> Jim Palmer

Day 3: Loss of Language

Religion provides language for considering life and communicating about deep issues. Language is so important, John wanted us to view Jesus as the manifested speech of the divine, calling him "Logos":

In the beginning was the Word, and the Word was with God, and the Word was God.

Christians rely on phrases from scripture when trying to comfort a friend or bolster their own courage. Christian communities employ jargon in addition to Bible verses. Your own circle might use phrases like "feeling convicted," "submitting," "knowing something in your heart," "letting go and letting God," or countless others.

During deconstruction, we begin recognizing problems with how we've used language, and in losing that lexicon, we may no longer know how to explain things, even to ourselves.

As you explore the idea of how humanity and divinity interconnect from outside the constraints of your denominational formation, you'll need new language. You may no longer want to pray "in Jesus' name," or call God "Father." You might even become uncomfortable with less specific terms, like "faith." But this isn't a bad thing. Fumbling for language helps us figure out what we think. Instead of having a phrase immediately handy, we must break down our thoughts and find the words which describe them. Some terms will feel right and true, others will feel clumsy. As you engage with others on the path, you'll encounter new phrases which you'll incorporate into your growing lexicon.

In any new environment it takes time to learn vocabulary, so while it might feel scary, it's going to be okay. Language is important, and it evolves. Just like you.

Change your opinions, keep your principles. Change your leaves, keep intact your roots.
Victor Hugo

Day 4: Loss of Relationships

A network of relationships is developed within church community, and the situation is like divorce, when friends choose with which partner to remain in relationship, because they can't figure out a way to maintain both. Some people won't be able to handle you turning away from things which made up a big part of their understanding of you. Others may fear your views could be contagious, or that you've been seduced by darkness which might target them next.

You might also discover you no longer *want* to spend time with people who use phrases, judgements, and thought patterns you've left behind. There's a possibility you could even lose your spouse or partner, though many couples find ways to navigate the difficulties of diverging belief systems.

When relationships can't survive your unlearning, the best you can do is release them with grace. Who knows what shifts await in their own spiritual journeys? They may end up circling back into your life as time passes. And if not, you can still wish them well and offer a blessing despite your sadness or anger. Your grace will speak loudly about how godliness outside of the Christianity they understand can look.

The pain of loss is real and valid, and you need to let yourself feel it to move forward. You have my prayers as you traverse your way through relationship shifts and loss. May the new connections heading into your life be rewarding and full of love.

Christians, especially evangelicals and fundamentalists, have a challenging relationship with reality. They insist that unprovable things are objectively true. And they deny things that have been proven to be objectively true. And both of these are litmus tests for membership.
Matt Nightingale

DAY 5: LOSS OF CERTAINTY

Since the beginning of time, people have asked questions about how planet Earth came into being, how humans appeared on it, and why death, suffering, and evil exist. Sacred myths in all religious traditions attempt to answer these questions. We endlessly strive to *know*, even though it's impossible to access fully true answers.

Humans love certainty. Not having answers makes us intensely uncomfortable, and so people all over the globe develop mythology which expands to include the whims and angers of gods or God, and the rituals and conduct required to assuage their varying thirsts.

Christianity follows the same path, and denominations center around answers to essential questions, such as what God wants, how to get to heaven, the way to treat "sinners," the proper form and meaning of baptism, the correct view of scripture, and many other issues. Countless denominational splits occur because groups of people are certain they hold the correct view while an opposing group believes differently.

The whole system seems to depend on certainty, and part of what faces you now is how to get comfortable with its loss. It's easier to quickly plop a label on something and slot it into a category than it is to co-exist, wrestle with, or simply contemplate complexity. Resting in unknowing, in mystery, feels scary.

Here's the good news: it gets easier. The more you release the idea that you know things you don't actually know, the simpler it gets. Meanwhile, the existence of Truth is always with you.

> *It saddens me to see seminarians and pastors equating a rigid hyper-orthodoxy with "holiness". There's a dangerous conflation of "being right" with "being righteous" and a tendency to make idols of our rituals, practices and doctrines, to show "we have God and you don't".*
> *We also want gold stars for our Justice and advocacy work and proofs of our "wokenesss." It isn't just the religious who create idols.*
> Rev. Daniel Brereton

Day 6: Loss of a Sense of Mission

Humans seem to function best when we have a sense of mission. It gives us things to focus our attention on, outlets for our energy, and ways to spend time which might otherwise be lonely. We long to be of service in tangible ways, and our day-to-day jobs often don't feel like they make the world a better place.

Stepping away from volunteer work at church can mean losing that sense of purpose. Pastors, priests, teachers in Christian schools and colleges, and leaders in faith-based initiatives experience this more intensely as both their belief systems and their jobs crumble.

The pain of aimlessness is real, and the sensation of idleness can feel like it should be immediately filled. But as with other losses you may need to rest in the emptiness for a bit. In agriculture, fields are regularly left fallow while those around them are sown and cultivated, so they can recover from the demands of fruit bearing. The same is true for human beings.

While you can find forms of volunteering outside the realm of faith, consider taking a moment to let your mind, body, and spirit lie fallow. God does deep work in the desert places. When we rush to replace what has finished, we run the risk of missing out on the transformative work of replenishment and revelation. We miss out on the turning of mental and emotional seasons where new things are given the chance to be dreamed into being.

Deconstruction may cost you your current ideas of mission. But the loss could result in an entirely new understanding of what the world needs, and how you can be a part of helping provide it.

> *Knowing our personal mission further enhances the flow of mysterious coincidences as we are guided toward our destinies. First we have a question, then dreams, daydreams, and intuitions lead us toward the answers, which usually are synchronistically provided by the wisdom of another human being.*
> James Redfield

Day 7: Loss of Sacraments

Views about the importance of sacraments largely depend on the tradition in which faith is formed. Roman Catholics and Orthodox traditions have seven sacraments: baptism, confirmation, confession (also called reconciliation), the Eucharist or communion, anointing of the sick, holy orders, and marriage. The United Methodist Church, Southern Baptists, Presbyterian Church USA, and other organizations recognize only baptism and communion.

If you've been part of a liturgical tradition, Eucharist/communion has likely been a central experience of church, and losing that visceral connection with God can be deeply painful. Struggles range from wondering how you'll be able to receive it if you leave your church, to questioning the whole idea of God appearing as bread and wine. Both questions are powerful and valid. Similar feelings can arise from the loss of going to confession.

Our spirits hunger for the idea of the transformative touch of God which feeds and cleanses us.

If you've left a congregation which no longer fits but still hunger for communion or confession, you can receive the sacraments in another church or denomination. Episcopal churches celebrate the Eucharist weekly (or more), and many of their priests offer to hear confession. Some Lutheran churches do as well.

If you're feeling stunned by the potential that the divine doesn't enter into sacramental actions because you've unlearned so much other church stuff, maybe you can set that fear aside for now. The God who calls you out of limited views of divinity is vastly bigger than the one most denominations permit. And a God who is larger must be vastly more able to inhabit bread and wine, water and salt, even you and I.

You can deconstruct your faith, reject church as you've known it, and still keep the sacraments if you want to. This is *your* journey.

A sacrament is physical, and within it is God's love; as a sandwich is physical, and nutritious and pleasurable, and within it is love, if someone makes it for you and gives it to you with love; even harried or tired or impatient love, but with love's direction and concern, love's again and again wavering and distorted focus on goodness; then God's love too is in the sandwich.
Andre Dubus II

Day 8: Loss of the Holy Family

Christians from Roman Catholic and Orthodox traditions often feel a connection to Mary and Joseph, given the importance of their role in the Christian narrative. You might have a special devotion to the holy family yourself, perhaps praying the Rosary and asking that Mary add your prayers to those she brings to God. Deconstructing your relationship with these figures can involve an intense sense of loss.

But maybe the focus can shift as you sift through the rubble of your understanding. Even if you don't view Jesus the way you used to, maybe the representation of his family can still resonate with meaning: about the importance of individuals and their decisions, about willingness to do hard things, about openness to the call of the divine even though it goes against all you've been taught.

Maybe you can hold on to a special identification with these people for whom life was entirely disrupted. People of deep faith, whose understanding of God was suddenly rent in pieces.

Maybe we can see ourselves in their vulnerability and acceptance, cradling this tender new thing in our arms and trusting it will be a source of profound, surprising insight into the divine.

Deconstruction is a multifaceted experience which involves loss. It's up to us to decide which things we lose, and which we mold into something newer, something rounder, something deeper.

> *When we are securely rooted in personal intimacy with the source of life, it will be possible to remain flexible without being relativistic, convinced without being rigid, willing to confront without being offensive, gentle and forgiving without being soft, and true witnesses without being manipulative.*
> Henri J.M. Nouwen

Day 9: Loss of Identity

Richard Rohr uses the term "sacred wound" to describe the sufferings of life which propel spiritual growth. These wounds can come from external events—the death of a loved one, abuse, experiences of injustice, or countless other causes—but they can also come from strikes to our ego. When certainty about our mastery over faith and knowledge of God are threatened, it may result in identity crises which can act as one of these wounds.

The things we've discussed in this section—relationships, vocation or avocation, community, a sense of purpose—all contribute to a sense of identity, and when we lose them, we start to wonder who we are in their absence. Who are we without our circle of friends? Who are we without a mission? Who are we without the tasks we do to help others? Who are we if there is no God to call us beloved?

As you go through these questions you may feel overwhelmed by a sensation of unmooring, not simply to the structures, liturgies, and roles which church provides, but even from yourself.

Separating from a previous understanding of self can be a very painful loss because it's so deeply connected to our ego. But the pain is a form of Rohr's sacred wound which leads to spiritual growth. Unless we amputate the false notions of self we can't be free to find the true.

Ministry can indeed be a witness to the living truth that the wound, which causes us to suffer now, will be revealed to us later as the place where God intimated [God's] new creation.
Henri J. M. Nouwen

Things Biblish

The collection of books known as Christian scripture is the basis for actions and beliefs both beautiful and monstrous, and many Christians are taught to interact with them as if the writings themselves are divine. In the coming days we'll take a closer look at some views about the Bible to help inform your own evaluation.

Day 10: The Bible as False Idol

Much of the Christian world relies on the Bible as the chief (or only) way of reaching God. In many circles the Christian scriptures have been elevated to near divinity, with a confusion of the Word of God (Jesus) with the word of God (holy writings). This view tries to cram a fourth person into the Holy Trinity, making the Bible an idol, despite the practice of idolatry being condemned in the very pages they worship.

But scriptures are meant to be icons rather than idols, and icons are ancient forms of artwork designed to be windows into heaven through prayer. They aren't meant to be so much looked *at* as looked *through* to behold the glorious mysteries of God. This is what the Bible should be, but often isn't.

Our search for a deeper understanding of God can't begin and end in a book. It begins in our hearts; with all its hungers and outpourings. It expands with wonder at the fractals of flowers and expands into the majesty of the universe, all of these things offering insight into Love if we care and dare to look.

Even for the most devout pre-deconstruction Christian, the Bible should act as an icon of God; a window through which to contemplate the meaning of life and holiness. If you've viewed it as a concrete and definitive container of the divine, or worse yet, God themself, it's time to let that go.

God, when the Bible fails us as an idol, when it fails us as a substitute for
You and a substitute for intimacy: please draw our tired souls to Jesus.
Amen.
Laura Jean Truman

Day 11: The "Bible Alone" Myth

The idea that some believers are "Bible alone" Christians is a falsehood, because so many things faith groups teach don't come from Christian scriptures. More importantly, the Bible itself never claims to be the only place to look for revelation and truth about God. The closest it comes is in this verse:

Every Scripture is God-breathed and profitable for teaching, for reproof, for correction, and for instruction in righteousness, that each person who belongs to God may be complete, thoroughly equipped for every good work.
(2 Timothy 3:16-17)

As you can see, the passage describes scripture as "profitable" (sometimes translated as "useful") rather than "required." It doesn't say there are no other ways of teaching, reproving, correcting, and instructing. Surely if Paul thought it was the sole method, he would have included the sentiment in his writings to Timothy and the nascent churches scattered throughout the region.

Paul didn't proclaim a Bible-alone approach to godliness, and more importantly, neither did Jesus. But somewhere along the line much of Christianity concluded that revelation about God beyond what is presented in scripture isn't valid, as if a single collection of written words can possibly contain the fullness of truth about any subject, let alone the force which powers the universe.

If God can only communicate to us through the words of one book, then God is a character inside that book and we do not live inside his story. God is not just a character inside the Bible but a fire with infinite voices who give stories to people of every nation.
Morgan Guyton

Day 12: What Did Jesus Say?

Matthew 5 offers a Reader's Digest Condensed version of the Christ mind. After Jesus speaks about the blessedness of those who suffer, mourn, and hunger for righteousness, he chastises the faux holiness of a group of religious zealots. He then goes on to offer revisions to various scriptures about anger, lust, divorce, vengeance, vows, and love for enemies. ("You have heard it said that… but I say…")

Jesus repeatedly told his followers that a scripture-constrained idea of righteousness needed adjusting, but here we are millennia later with a similarly rule-bound, book-based system rather than a Way of Love.

The parables are filled with stories about religious understandings turned upside down. Workers arriving late but paid full wages. Prodigal sons being welcomed. Disdained people like Samaritans held up as models for love of neighbor. Jesus broke numerous laws related to ritual cleanliness and the Sabbath. In the tales he told, the instructions he offered, and in his actions, Jesus demonstrated that our interpretation of scripture was seriously flawed. The idea that we should follow it as a rule book rather than something deeper, more meaning-filled, and transformational is profoundly unscriptural.

Nazarene
Say that he was legend,
The dream of slaves and beggars,
Or hippy poet so charged
With music of the spheres
That stones sang beneath his naked feet.
I care not if he lived
Or uttered any word,
Or healed a single leper.
I know only that his name
Reveals that gift of pain
That only love can bear
And having borne still cry
"I love."
Pauli Murray

Day 13: Colonization of Scripture

A social media pundit proselytized that Christianity "claims the 'Old Testament.'" There are problems with this view on many levels.

The phrase "Old Testament" is a quintessentially colonialist view. The collection of books Christians call OT were the Hebrew scriptures then and continue to be now, but that reality is ignored or erased by Christian appropriation.

The thread continued:

The Scriptures are all Christological. At face-value they at times need to be subverted (which Christ, Paul, etc. did), but this is only to reveal their meaning all along.

Jewish people do not view their holy books as containing Jesus in every story. And aren't they the experts? Shouldn't Christians defer to Jewish understanding, rather than imprinting on it the things we want to see written there?

Within these conversational circles, the Hebrew and Christian holy books are referred to with a capital S, or simply as *"the* scriptures." This designation nullifies the existence of holy writings for countless other religious traditions. People can believe their view of God is more accurate than other religions offer, but that doesn't mean they should erase the existence of other scriptures.

Our deconstruction process should include rejection of colonialist views and behaviors, and reparation for the damage our views have done. Humanity's desire to capture the stories of our search for God is not limited to the followers of Jesus. Scriptural traditions for all religions are worthy of respect.

In our one small and interwoven world, the great spiritual messengers of all the sacred traditions are a universal human treasure, to be received and reverenced with the respect due an attained being, an exemplar of a higher level of human consciousness.
Cynthia Bourgeault

Day 14: Experience is Important

The gospels are full of stories about people experiencing the divine presence in transcendent ways. Encounters with the love Jesus manifested transformed people and changed the world.

While an experiential understanding of God has been explored by mystics throughout the centuries, many contemporary Christian streams reject the idea, believing the days of engagement are over, and that the only way to access divine truth is by reading the Bible. People are told they are "living epistles" as an exhortation for good behavior because others are watching. But using the term this way ignores something critical; the reality that God is still engaging with us. We are living epistles because the story of humanity's search for God never ends. The writing continues.

Experience is important. It's the difference between gazing at a picture of a loved one and hugging them. And it matters on both sides. When we seek the divine and encounter moments of transcendence, God is receiving us too. When we magnify divine love through our actions, others experience God, through us. We are all love letters to each other and the world.

The "good news" is only good if it is perpetually unfolding, so that all people can participate in that kind of active exchange of love. God never stops experiencing us. Let's not deny ourselves the potential experience of them.

The entire canon of Scripture is overflowing with experiences. Scripture is stories about experiences with God.
Tina Osterhouse

Day 15: Inerrancy and Infallibility

God calls our hearts to search for them, and the call inspires people to capture stories. As the centuries have unfolded, Christians decided that the divine inspiration to write down one people's collection of stories should be deemed different from all others, and that God themselves directly controlled the telling of the tales collected in Hebrew and Christian scripture. The books were declared to be inerrant and infallible. There was essentially a deification of the very process of writing, with God's breath bearing magical properties of protection from human error.

This concept forces people who read the Bible to manage cognitive dissonance for statements like "God is love" co-existing with passages in which God orders the murder of babies. Most Christians dismiss their confusion, saying "we can't understand the mysteries of God," "God's ways are higher than our ways," and "doesn't the painter have the right to destroy his paintings?" But deconstruction gives us the opportunity to address serious biblical questions.

If we grapple with the reality of how the divine is described in the Bible, we're forced to make a decision. Either God is a vindictive being with multiple personalities, or we ascribed a whole bunch of natural disasters and bad human behavior to an entity who wasn't actually orchestrating those events. If God is love, which of these two potentials seems more likely?

Imagine how frustrated you would be if your willful 13-year-old child wrote your biography, bringing up the worst moments of your relationship and attributing all sorts of negative character traits to you, and the world embraced that book and proclaimed that that's who you are. Now imagine how frustrated God must be.

The Spirit inspires humans in all kinds of ways; through the arts, acts of kindness, insights into the divine nature, and so much more. The original writers of scripture could be inspired by the whispers of God and still not convey divinity's full intent or meaning. There is room for inspiration to result in inaccuracy. There is room for life and movement within our understanding of scripture than much of Christianity admits and permits.

But creation shouts the truth; God is incomprehensibly bigger than any book, any church, or any religion.

> *Sense perceptions can be and often are false and deceptive, however real they may appear to us. Where there is realization outside the senses, it is infallible. It is proved not by extraneous evidence but in the transformed conduct and character of those who have felt the real presence of God within.*
> Mahatma Gandhi

Day 16: Bible as Parable

After wrestling with the questions raised in yesterday's contemplation, I finally came to a new comfort with the harsh tales of a murderous and vengeful god. That new view was inspired in part by one of Jesus' favorite modes of teaching: through storytelling.

From the earliest days of humanity, individuals were inspired to pass down tales which we can now quite rightly view as ridiculous misassignment of blame, and misunderstanding about who God is. It's easier and more dramatic to blame catastrophes on the bad behavior of our neighbors who deserve a divine spanking than it is to offer in-depth evaluation of complex ecological, economic, and social interconnections which lead to famine, slavery, stolen land, and plague. Not to mention the ancient peoples had no access to the tools of today which permit closer examination of cause and effect.

But hear me out: perhaps we're not meant to read them that way. Perhaps we should read the tales as part of an extended parable. Perhaps they are a way of teaching by negative example.

Chapter 14 of John's gospel offers a glimpse into the Christmind as a conversation between Phillip and Jesus unfolds. Jesus repeats a central theme: that if we see and hear him, we see and hear the Creator. The essential message seems to boil down to Christ telling us we got our understanding of divinity wrong until then, and that we should pay attention and follow this new idea of what a God of love looks like.

Let yourself consider the idea that the violent, vicious, vindictiveness we read in the ancient stories can indeed teach us… but by negative example.

Things Biblish

We can't know full truths about God; if we could they wouldn't be God. Let yourself recognize that humans were wrong about divine causation when they captured the tales thousands of years ago, continue to be wrong as we try to explain the stories now, and will always be wrong until we breathe synchronously with the divine breath.

> *The long painful history of the Church is the history of people ever and again tempted to choose power over love, control over the cross, being a leader over being led. Those who resisted this temptation to the end and thereby give us hope are the true saints.*
> Henri Nouwen

Day 17: Seek Incandescence

In the first section of this book, we discussed the reality that one of the losses deconstructing Christians experience is the comfort and ritual of turning to the pages of the Bible for study, solace, or as a preface to prayer. As our understanding of God, faith, and church change shape, the scripture we previously esteemed so highly begins to tarnish, and it becomes increasingly easy to view it with disdain.

We're taught to look to biblical rules and regulations and seek promises of what we'll get for good behavior. What we aren't taught is how to look for the incandescent bits.

In my *Sex With God* devotional, I describe scripture as the veils of a seductive dancer which offer enticing peeks at the person performing the dance. The point isn't to focus on the veils, but on what is hidden behind them. Certainly there are pieces of the Bible which will never make anyone other than a genealogist shiver, but as you move through deconstruction, you may find that a new way of reading is revealed. When we stop looking at Christian scripture as an end to itself and "the" portal to God, and view it instead as a shimmering image which has something more profound and beautiful dancing behind it, we might find that our relationship with the text transforms and deepens.

Those who penned stories about the faith heroes, Jesus, and the early church had no idea we'd use their words the way we do now. But the divine dance can't be stopped despite our attempts to cover it like an old-fashioned nun. The cosmic seduction can be glimpsed through the Bible if we let our minds drift and our eyes droop sleepily, losing focus on rules, regulations, and reason, and opening ourselves to mystery and vision.

Both things are there, if we dare to seek them.

I have always been a person of prayer. Even as an atheist, and even during my deconstruction of faith, I always found prayer as a habit. I suppose I've sort of always sensed there was something more even when I hated the church. My life of prayer these days lingers somewhere between Pentecostal, mystic, and ritual Catholic contemplative silence. I've studied with rabbis and Buddhist monks, shamans and pagans to understand more their own rituals of prayer.

There is something almost cellular to me in prayer. It's like I'm always doing it; even when I'm having to sweep the floor and clean the toilet. And even more so, when I am surrounded by the majesty of nature.

Sure, temples, cathedrals, and chapels are great; but I'd rather be surrounded by the liturgy of lakes and larks, and the litany of the living world and land. Even in bird song, I hear echoes of divine speech and sacred wisdom.

Bec Cranford

THINGS CHURCHISH

Western culture's Christian roots run deep, penetrating virtually every social issue of our era. In this section we'll take a look at common problematic aspects of church structure and operation.

Day 18: Church as False Idol

For many years I thought the optimal model for church would be a system of individual congregations all working together to move believers where they best fit. Seeker-friendly churches would be the beginning for many, with people "graduating" to places with additional layers of theology or liturgy; each person's faith becoming richer, deeper, and more complex as they progressed. Each church having a pool of people entering and being fed, right where they were.

Unfortunately that system isn't possible, because so much of Christianity is about othering, isolating, and sheep-retaining. Too many denominations are filled with preachers proclaiming a One True Belief system, and clinging to tithers as if their paychecks rely on it. (Because they do.) Weekly church attendance is described as "obligation" in Roman Catholicism, and Southern Baptists look askance if you don't show up Sunday mornings and Wednesday nights.

Many churches act as systems for reproving individuals or families, judging behaviors and issuing proclamations of justice. The institution is held up as *the* way to God, the only accurate interpreter of scripture, and the place you damn well better go if you want to be saved.

But that's the opposite of what Jesus told people about bringing the kingdom of heaven to earth.

Institutional Christianity has become a golden calf, and the best way to see the glowing light of the divine is to stop staring into the glare of idols.

> *The entire purpose of Western constructive theology is to construct a frame monstrous enough to push us beyond itself—that we might awaken to that which is experientially beyond any categorization, rationality, or frame. The point is to move us through the apophatic threshold.*
> Tim Burnette

Day 19: Clergy as Mini Gods

Christians want ministers to be pure, spotless, and holy, and want them to align with our individual views of what holiness means. In Roman Catholicism priests are believed to be standing "in persona Christi" (meaning "in the person of God") when they offer communion, forgive sins, preach, teach, and shepherd. In this view, Christ is actually performing these things as long as the priest was ordained through approved apostolic succession.

In high church traditions, clergy are garbed in ornate robes which shine a spotlight on the idea of exalted holiness. They glow in white and gold, burn in red, exude royalty in purple, and promise life in green. In other traditions, pastors pare vestments down to stoles worn over simple robes, more modest in their separation, though still apart. But we elevate our ministers to omniscient omnipotence even without the glittering raiment.

This humans-as-idols model wasn't what Jesus demonstrated. The apostles served together with the disciples, and their flaws were on display for all to see (and for Jesus to point out). Jesus never preached an episcopal structure or a priesthood of them-versus-us. Generations of Christ followers created their own structure of priests and elders, scribes, factions, and denominations, with each group holding different views on what it means to be holy.

In Matthew 16, Jesus rebuked Peter for demanding God shouldn't be vulnerable enough to be crucified, saying such a view was human rather than divine. If this is true for the Christ himself, how much truer must it be for the humans who seek to serve him as ministers in the world today?

Having an expectation of super holiness tempts clergy who struggle with pride, and neglects clergy who struggle with emotional, familial, or personal issues. Hyper expectation discourages everyday folk who want to love and serve God but feel they aren't good enough, and causes ministers to be banished or quit because they can't meet impossible standards.

Things Churchish

What if instead of deifying pastors, faith communities welcomed them as flawed co-laborers, fully human and charged with specific tasks for a congregation, but no more capable of bearing divine truth than you and I?

What if we could truly call these ministers "friends" as Jesus did with his full knowledge of the apostles' strengths and weaknesses, looking across to see them rather than up?

What if clergy were allowed to share their areas of brokenness with us as freely as we share ours with them?

What might Christianity become if we destroyed "clergyolotry" and instead served together with transparency, truth and freedom?

How much easier might we find encountering the divine if we seek together as siblings?

Ministry means the ongoing attempt to put one's own search for God, with all the moments of pain and joy, despair and hope, at the disposal of those who want to join this search but do not know how.
Henri Nouwen

Day 20: Whose Words are Whose?

Let the words of my mouth and the meditation of my heart
be acceptable in your sight,
O Lord, my rock and my redeemer.
Psalm 19:14 ESV

You've probably heard this prayer kicking off a sermon at some point in your church attendance, and may even have heard weekly. It's a good prayer for those who teach or preach, but it can also act as a catchall request that whatever they dreamed up for the Sunday reflection be blessed, whether wisdom or nonsense.

There are thousands of wonderful clergy who sincerely hope to convey love and truth through their words. Unfortunately, because pastors and priests are people too, there are also many who get high on admiration and end up conflating their thoughts with God's.

One symptom of this problem is the practice of sizing sermon notes to fit within a Bible, and then using the book to hold and hide those notes. The person giving the sermon glances down to see what words come next. Meanwhile, people in the pews watch, and from their vantage point, the preacher looks as if they're reading from the Bible. This happens frequently in Evangelical circles, where Christian scripture is elevated to divine levels, or at least, it used to before the era of electronic tablets.

Do most people recognize what's actually happening? Of course. But the situation is thorny regardless. If pastors believe Hebrew scripture, the gospels, and the epistles to be the literal word of God, then they should do everything in their power to ensure their flock knows the difference between the Bible and their own notes. If you attend a church in which the pastor uses the Bible as a folio for their sermon notes, consider letting them know it's problematic.

May the meditations of all our hearts be pleasing to the creator of the universe. Amen and amen. But let's acknowledge that our ability to know truth is limited, and that the things we convey should be cloaked in humility rather than treated as having come directly from God.

> *Heaven is intimacy with the divine, which is always a present tense event until it becomes the only presence we experience. We cannot earn our way into heaven; we can only stumble into it.*
> Morgan Guyton

Day 21: Hotbed for Abuse

Church culture creates a fertile climate for abuse of many kinds. Idolizing clergy means certain people are viewed unquestioningly, their actions above scrutiny or reproach. The hierarchy of holiness descending down from clergy through the leadership structure results in tiers of perceived trustworthiness, whether deserved or not. People who donate large amounts of money can be given authority and power largely because of their financial contributions. Purity culture adds another problematic layer, where sexual abuse results in victim shaming.

Abuse can include emotional manipulation, sexual exploitation, "conversion therapy," exclusion or shame due to divorce, and many other wrongs.

Just before 9/11 I entered a church broken and hurting in more ways than I could count. I arrived full of skills coupled with unmet emotional needs and a hunger for approval. The priest and his wife became my friends, I thought. Good friends. Close friends. Meanwhile, my pain was eased by the gospel I heard, the hours of service I offered, and the increasing words of affirmation and attention from the priest which ultimately transformed into something emotionally and sexually twisted.

I was enraptured. I was taken advantage of. I was spiritually abused.

It's taking years to unpack the extent of the exploitation, to reject self-blame, and to see how wide the roots of wrongdoing spread within that specific congregation, more widely in the denomination, and on out into church structures generally.

My story is not unusual. People experience abuse in church settings all too frequently. Some organizations are more rife for it than others, but the truth is that climates of hierarchical power including "divine" ordination for the caretaking of souls creates an ecosystem of components which feed exploitation and abuse.

Groups of people coming together to seek an understanding of divinity, support each other, and to work toward social justice have the potential for doing tremendous good. But given humanity's proclivity for bad behavior, it's hard to know how to create such an entity which is free of problematic power dynamics.

> *The devil doesn't look like red lights and songs about sex. He looks like a trusted pastor telling you he's sorry, he's not going to report your attacker to the police, your attacker is just too important to the ministry—and are you sure the attack wasn't really your fault?*
> Josiah Hawthorne

Day 22: Childish Things

When I was a child, I spoke as a child, I felt as a child, I thought as a child. Now that I have become a man, I have put away childish things. For now we see in a mirror, dimly, but then face to face. Now I know in part, but then I will know fully, even as I was also fully known.
(1 Corinthians 13:11-12)

There's so much richness in these words from Paul to the people of Corinth. We can imagine him thinking back to stoning those who dared believe God inhabited human flesh, cared more for mercy than justice, and violated many rules understood to be requirements for righteousness. Paul seems to have assessed his past violence and lack of enlightenment as childish and viewed the expansion of his understanding as maturity.

Paul's words didn't stop there, however. He went on to admit that he still didn't know it all, and wouldn't until his spirit was separated from its complex cage of thorny flesh.

Paul's journey is a reflection of the deconstruction process, which begins with childish acceptance of our church's teaching before transforming into something deeper, richer, and truer. Progress often mirrors the relationship we have with our parents. When we're little we view them as all powerful, all protecting, and all knowing. Our parents (and our faith system or church itself) are mini gods who sustain us, rule us, and keep us alive. But as we get older, we start questioning rules, decisions, and authority. We begin to realize that our mom and dad (and our understanding of God and church) have flaws. We start to see the cracks in our ideas of who and what they were. We may even walk away from our parents (or church) for a while, unable to reconcile their marred reality with our need for something more perfect.

But humans—and human understanding of the divine—are all flawed.

Things Churchish

When we move past the pain of loss and anger we put away childish things. The relationship an adult can have with a parent has depth and sweetness which are impossible during childhood. And the relationship we can have with God as a result of deconstruction has that same promise for being so much more full, sweet, and true.

> *If all will admit that all have an equal right to think, then the question is forever solved; but as long as organized and powerful churches, pretending to hold the keys of heaven and hell, denounce every person as an outcast and criminal who thinks for himself and denies their authority, the world will be filled with hatred and suffering.*
> Robert G. Ingersoll

Day 23: Having "Enough Faith"

In evangelical and fundamentalist circles there's a correlation presumed between the degree of faith you hold and the outcome of your prayers. Roman Catholic, Orthodox, Episcopal, and other liturgical traditions tend to focus on this less, but you may still have encountered the concept even within those denominations.

The concept shows itself in a variety of types of prayer. In charismatic circles, faith is required in prayers for healing, as if there's a divine measuring stick God uses and if you're an eighth of an inch short they won't dole out the necessary cosmic medicine. It's also connected to the "prosperity gospel," in which having enough faith and praying the right way ensures wealth and happiness.

But if faith is the controller of healing and wealth, why aren't the historic Christian heroes alive and bankrolling social justice reform?

Any god who permits themselves to be manipulated in this way can't actually be God. They're a genie in a book-shaped bottle which has to be rubbed the right way to get results. The ineffable mystery behind creation must be infinitely more generous, permissive of our will, and tuned into the ever-expanding universe than the petty bureaucrat so many of us envision.

God—who is love—is intensely attracted to and enamored by all of us, swooshing in to embrace each thought and question we have about who they might be.

There is no such thing as having "enough" faith. Our imaginations aren't big enough to hold the wonder of an actual God.

A lot of retired clergy are a hot mess with no faith left in humanity or God because they tried to be who the church asked them to be, instead of who God made them to be.
Rev. Heather Riggs

Day 24: A "Right Way" to Pray

Many of us were taught that prayers won't be answered unless we add "in Jesus' name" at the end, as if prayer was a magical incantation with the outcomes dependent on specific words and accurate pronunciations. The gospels show Jesus teaching the disciples how to pray, and in that prayer, there was zero mention of including his name. In John 15 and 16 he talks about God granting requests in his name, but there's never a statement that God *denies* prayers without that secret password. The idea is closely related to the magical thinking discussed yesterday and reduces God to a petty game player.

Consider this: if someone at a dinner party asks for the saltshaker, do you hand it to them or just go silent until they couple their request with your favorite nickname for yourself?

This is a silly illustration which conveys truth, but the issue might connect with a deconstruction fear that if we don't pray in Jesus' name, we'll lose Jesus himself: the person we think of as the very center of our faith. If we stop praying in his name, doesn't it put us at risk for losing the concept of his divinity? And will we be left bereft in the wake of its leaving?

The divine wants to be in conversation with us. We can hold on to a concept of Christ as the center of hope for healing lives separated from love, without having to cling to Jesus-centric formulas for prayer.

As a result of my deconstruction, when requesting blessings over food and offering other audible prayers, I conclude by saying "in your many names we pray."

How you phrase things is not terribly important. The desire to be in union *is*.

Jesus told him, "Don't be afraid; just believe."
Mark 5:36b NIV

Day 25: The Problem of "Mission"

Our contemporary understanding of mission and ministry creates a hierarchical structure of givers and receivers. The givers have something they assume the recipients don't have. That something could be information, material resources, or greater access to God. The structure inherently creates a situation of better than/less than which is a false reflection of reality, and a poor understanding of the centrality of relationship to the divine.

Jesus told the apostles to wash each other's feet, and instructed his followers to go and make disciples, not to create hierarchical church structures entirely dependent on a model of us vs. them presented as altruism. The story of Jesus' coming is itself instructional about this. Christian understanding is that God chose to manifest with us, as us, thereby striking down the idea of separateness.

Take a look at Jesus' instructions in this passage:

> *But they do all their works to be seen by men. They make their phylacteries broad and enlarge the fringes of their garments, and love the place of honor at feasts, the best seats in the synagogues, the salutations in the marketplaces, and to be called 'Rabbi, Rabbi by men. But you are not to be called 'Rabbi', for one is your teacher, the Christ, and all of you are brothers. Call no man on the earth your father, for one is your Father, he who is in heaven. Neither be called masters, for one is your master, the Christ. But he who is greatest among you will be your servant. Whoever exalts himself will be humbled, and whoever humbles himself will be exalted.*
> (Matthew 29:-12)

Christians often ignore everything except the last line, or use the preceding words to castigate Roman Catholics for calling priests father. The final sentence is critical, clearly, but it's interconnected with the sentences in which Jesus excoriates a group of people who wanted titles and prestige.

Things Churchish

Modern church falls prey to the same kind of pride, with swinging fringes and phylacteries transformed into towering pulpits and social media platforms. God cries woe upon them then, and on us today, for clinging to the hierarchy of ministry rather than reaching for a different model, a togetherness model, an all-of-us serving all-of-us model.

It's time to move away from "ministry" and into relationships of love and mutuality, with God and each other.

> *While we as people of God are certainly called to feed the hungry and clothe the naked, that whole "we're blessed to be a blessing" thing can still be kind of dangerous. It can be dangerous when we self-importantly place ourselves above the world, waiting to descend on those below so we can be the "blessing" they've been waiting for, like it or not.*
> Nadia Bolz-Weber

Day 26: Savior Complex

Savior complex is a psychological concept in which we identify ourselves as being central to the rescue of others. In a Christian context this can be limited to the notion of saving souls but can also extend to the idea that by sharing our testimony, spiritual practices, and understanding of righteousness, we can transform people's lives here and now.

You may have encountered priests, pastors, elders, Sunday school teachers, or musical worship leaders who dole out not just churchy advice, but also counsel on finance, marriage, and countless other issues for which they aren't qualified. You might even recognize the tendency in yourself.

Christians are trained to think "saving" others is a virtue of the highest order. It's a hard thing to unlearn, and can transition into family relationships and friendships, where boundaries about roles get confused and dysfunctional.

Wanting to help people is a good and sacred thing. But believing our understanding of God gives us divine authority to try to change other people is a problem. The savior complex is essentially a superiority complex, and as you deconstruct you'll need to resist its seduction. You may feel newly on fire to share your expanding understanding of the divine, and thereby "save" others from the limits and problems of Christianity as you've known it. But the best teachers are not dogmatic. Think about Yoda, the Karate Kid's Mr. Miyagi, and St. Francis of Assisi who suggested that we preach without words. Your inner calm and peace may do more to "save" people than all attempts to explain your new beliefs.

I feel unalterably angry about what we've done. What we continue to do. I don't think I'll ever stop being angry at the injustice of what white people have done to bodies in the name of whatever god we steal or create.
Jamie Lee Finch

Day 27: Colonization of Peoples

An offshoot of Christian savior complex's obsession with "mission" is colonization. A great deal of the takeover of indigenous cultures around the world took place during the 1600-1800s, and a number of nations are still held within colonial rule. A toxic mix of economic incentive and religious furor fueled "saviors" to travel the globe seeking money to be made and souls to be saved, and the ongoing ramifications of that zeal continue to unfold.

Here in the United States, we embraced the dogma of manifest destiny, believing that God actually desired for us to "subdue" native peoples, here and elsewhere. The resources of nations were raped, gorgeous indigenous understandings of gender, sexuality, and spirituality were decimated, and centuries-old ways of life were destroyed, all in the name of "good news".

Efforts to "save" people from their indigenous spiritual beliefs continue to thrive in fundamentalist and evangelical Christian communities. Believers are taught that persons who don't acknowledge Jesus as their personal Lord and savior are going to burn in hell, and that it's therefore the central Christian duty to send missionaries, Bibles, and shoe boxes filled with American junk and Jesus leaflets around the planet to browbeat heathens into heaven.

But how do these processes and outcomes align with the words Jesus offered to his disciples about what they should do and how they were to live? Sure he told them to go to all the nations and make disciples, teaching them to observe what he commanded (Matthew 28:19-20), but few Christians seem to pay attention to what those commands were, and it's a pretty limited list. First this:

> *A new commandment I give to you, that you love one another. Just as I have loved you, you also love one another. By this everyone will know that you are my disciples, if you have love for one another.*
> (John 13:34-35)

Then this:

Jesus said to him, "You shall love the Lord your God with all your heart, with all your soul, and with all your mind. This is the first and great commandment. A second likewise is this, 'You shall love your neighbor as yourself. The whole law and the prophets depend on these two commandments."
(Matthew 22:37-40)

The Jesus Christian missionaries proclaim Lord and savior commanded love, not submission. He never suggested the violence, extortion, and coercion which characterized so much of colonial Christian history.

All religions are humanity's attempt to glimpse the unglimpsable. We have much to learn from cultures we've badly injured. It's hard to know how to begin repairing that damage, but at the very least we should stop seeing ourselves as saviors of the world, and reconsider what "Christian mission" work we should and shouldn't support.

Until the lions have their own historians, the history of the hunt will always glorify the hunter.
Chinua Achebe

Day 28: Invisible Bars of Control

Whether intentionally or not, religion is frequently used as a tool of control. Denominational structures control who has power within their idea of church, how money is spent, who can become members, which genders can preach and serve, what constitutes "true" baptism, and countless other issues. Controlling the groupthink to ensure adherence keeps funds funneling in, and in the minds of many, keeps society spinning smoothly.

While the faithful within these institutions are generally unaware of the breadth of control being imposed, many feel a twinge of discomfort at issues which hit close to home. A woman may feel she's called to preach. A man may wish his Wednesday evenings were free for relaxation after a hard day. But both give in to expectations for the sake of peace and out of respect and subservience to the idea that those in church leadership have some kind of divine authority, and so their instructions must be good.

When we deconstruct, we awaken to realize the bars erected to control us are like the emperor's new clothes. They don't exist except through the insistence of those who created them and by our own complicity and permission.

Before his encounter with Christ on the road to Damascus, Saul/Paul was all about controlling people within the context of faith. His inability to quell the spread of Jesus' message led him to murder. He had to be struck blind in order to actually see. Waking up to recognize how wrong he'd been must have been painful. Pastors, ministers, and priests who wake up to the ways they've used control over Christ followers can be similarly painful, but similarly profound.

Your own journey may include a period in which you feel blind, helpless, and remorseful, as you recognize that the idea of controlling people is antithetical to a God who created us for freedom.

Freedom is dangerous to those who want to control outcomes. But the universe is full of danger and adventure, for those who dare proclaim that the bars are a lie.

> *The thing I know about Love is this: it seeks to understand. It does not value doctrine over relationship or humans. It is the thing we need most yet it is the thing religion starves us of. Religion cloaks love in law and guards it with pride.*
> Marie Lerch

How Tos

We've worked through a number of problematic topics and challenges related to deconstruction. But how can you deconstruct well? What can you do to get the most out of the process?

The coming days of reflection direct your focus toward progress.

Day 29: Pray for Wisdom

In the early phases of deconstruction, many people pray that the questions will just go away. Since you're reading this book, you've probably moved through that phase, but as we struggle through our clouds of uncertainty, it can be hard to know how to pray, or if we should even try to talk to God at all.

Let's look at an account of prayer from Hebrew scripture; the request of Solomon to be given wisdom:

"I am just a little child. I don't know how to go out or come in. Give your servant therefore an understanding heart to judge your people, that I may discern between good and evil; for who is able to judge this great people of yours?"

This request pleased the Lord, that Solomon had asked this thing. God said to him, "Because you have asked this thing, and have not asked for yourself long life, nor have you asked for riches for yourself, nor have you asked for the life of your enemies, but have asked for yourself understanding to discern justice; behold, I have done according to your word. Behold, I have given you a wise and understanding heart; so that there has been no one like you before you, and after you none will arise like you.
(1 Kings 3:7b, 9-12)

Solomon was far from perfect, as we see from some of the things that unfold later in his story. But these words show the pleasure God took from Solomon's desire to be able to rule the people justly.

No matter how furiously we stomp our feet and declare that particular words of the Bible mean *this*, and various teachings of our denominations mean *that*, we are all just little children, not knowing how to go in or out. We can all benefit from earnestly desiring the real wisdom which comes from having understanding hearts.

Wisdom is that deep truth which surpasses knowledge and any kind of silly concept of "right belief". Wisdom is seeing the deep, universal meaning in the words of scripture rather than parsing text as a means for creating rule systems.

So go ahead and lift a prayer, right now. Pray that you be given the wisdom of Solomon. Align your mind and heart to seeking truth. Be confident that when you earnestly seek truth, Truth will be very pleased to be found.

> *For the first time in my life I saw the truth as it is set into song by so many poets, proclaimed as the final wisdom by so many thinkers. The truth - that Love is the ultimate and highest goal to which man can aspire. Then I grasped the meaning of the greatest secret that human poetry and human thought and belief have to impart: The salvation of man is through love and in love.*
> Viktor E. Frankl

Day 30: Remember Humility

I had a conversation with an evangelical Christian once in which I tried to explain my view that God was bigger than could be expressed through the pages of the Bible or held within a human mind. They responded by saying my view was prideful. The idea puzzled me, because it's the opposite of pride to acknowledge there are things you don't know.

What they *actually* meant was that I lacked submissiveness to their particular sets of beliefs. But that's not pride.

Humility is an essential part of learning. If we insist we already know something, it's extremely hard to open our brains to new ideas. The harder we demand we know who and what God is, the less likely we are to allow revelation which the divine endlessly hungers to pour into us. Even *good* ideas about God can get in the way of our experiencing God, and therefore better understanding the divine. The broader ideas you might increasingly embrace could very well become stumbling blocks to an even more expansive understanding.

Pride is the enemy of so many things. It's particularly destructive in relationships, and God desires us to not so much acquire knowledge about them, but to be in relationship with them. When we relinquish rule-bound ideas of holiness, we recognize not only that we don't have answers, we don't even know the right questions.

We also need to let go of the idea that we aren't good enough to be in the divine presence. It's always there. We are neither good enough, nor not good enough. We are both. We are neither. But regardless, we are carriers of the divine spark of love, light, and joy.

As you continue your deconstruction journey, try to sit in a place of humble boldness. Develop an attitude of openness and availability, of simple waiting. Acknowledge the reality that there are things too deep to understand.

God will meet you in that space.

In the midst of excitement, grief, joy, and solitude, I remind myself every moment that the sole mission of my life is to find 'the ultimate questioner' - that unimaginable who has put me in this madness to answer an unanswerable question.
Kedar Joshi

Day 31: Ask Why You Believe What You Do

Why do you believe what you believe?

This is an important question, and one you may need to sit with for a bit to answer.

Did it come from preaching? Did it come from Sunday school teaching? Did it come from revelation?

For virtually all Christians, we ascribe to a set of concepts because someone taught them to us. Our hearts may have been transformed by joy, sorrow, or some other experience of God which started us on our journey, and those experiences can be unshakable bedrock. But when it comes to the complex and interwoven system of religion and faith, most of it is supplied by other people who tell us what the Bible is, what kinds of sin destroys the soul, and whether it's okay to dance, drink wine, love a person of the same sex, divorce, or live gender authentically.

The issue of *why* we believe what we do is critically important. If our goal is to reach for the divine, why do we permit our faith to be structured and constrained by humans?

Given how much of our faith comes from what is taught by people rather than in the endless mystery of God, why are we so afraid to untether ourselves from those teachings?

Humans are carriers of the divine, but none of us are God. Relax in this truth and permit yourself the freedom of releasing any teaching which reduces rather than widens your perception of the divine.

Don't miss out on a life full of passion and purpose because you're waiting for your mind to catch up with your heart.
Brooke Hampton

Day 32: Stop Striving

Contemplation is a spiritual practice which attempts to unite your spirit with God rather than engaging in intellectual conversation through prayer. Contemplative practices can be helpful during the deconstruction process, when our minds reel with questions.

The meditative position of sitting on the floor with legs crossed, palms upturned and resting on the knees has physical and metaphorical importance. It indicates openness; the palms ready to receive but not grasping, the chest and abdomen presented rather than protected, head up, available. This posture reminds us of what we should also be doing in spirit. Rather than striving, we need to simply make ourselves available.

When starting contemplation, you might find yourself struggling not to think, or be distracted by noises or concerns, or worried you aren't "doing it right." The conventional wisdom for managing our busy brains during contemplation is to acknowledge each thought or feeling when it comes, letting it go, and then simply resting your mind again.

The contemplative approach can be applied through ordinary moments of the day. It's merely an attitude of being available, of acknowledging the reality that God is there with you, in the space around you, and inside you. There is no need for striving. There is no need to grasp at what God is trying to "reveal" to you. It's like lying drowsily in bed with a beloved, simply enjoying their presence, with no need for conversation, no anticipation of sex, nothing other than just being together in the same space. A simple, non-expectant intimacy.

Stop demanding revelation, and simply rest in the truth that God is there. Be with them. If we keep demanding to define the divine, God will respect our orneriness and leave us to it. When we let go of intellectual concepts of God, we are in a better position to receive experiences of them.

One of the oldest longings of all people of mystical sensibility is to be rid of disguises to the point of becoming naked.
Dorothee Soelle

Day 33: Resist the Urge to Blame

In the early days of this book we talked about losses, and loss can lead to anger. You might feel like the casualty of something but aren't even sure what that thing is. It's natural to feel anger as part of your deconstruction experience.

We default to blaming someone when feeling discomfort. It might be our parents if they were the first formers of our faith, or other instrumental teachers of our religious understanding. We might be angry at entire church communities with whom we shared important moments of our lives, for instilling many things we now need to unravel and discard. It's possible you're also angry at the person or things which triggered your deconstruction process and launched the subsequent questions, doubts, worries, and pain.

It's hard to release, but the energy pushed into resenting others gets in the way of your ability to receive what comes next. (Abuse is, of course, an entirely different issue, and cases of it should be reported through appropriate channels and/or those with the highest likelihood of resulting in consequences for perpetrators.)

Anger is often an easier emotion to manage than feelings of helplessness or sorrow. But try to resist the urge to blame people. We are all on the perilous journey of life, all prone to centering our understanding of the world around our own knowledge, and all predisposed to sharing what we believe to "help" others. Christians are trained to actively spread their flavor of good news, and for most, do so with no ill intent.

The pain you're experiencing now is due to a complex mix of circumstances and scenarios. It's not any one person's or institution's fault. Release them with peace so you are free to wade deeper into the waters of life.

The secret of change is to focus all of your energy, not on fighting the old, but on building the new.
D. Millman

Day 34: Listen for the Divine Whisper

Jesus described a mutual knowing, saying his sheep knew his voice, and that he knew them. He spoke of other sheep who didn't hear that voice, didn't know it, and didn't follow it. But how do we hear and know the divine voice?

Our fascinating minds are constantly awhirl with thoughts and voices, urging us toward exploration or caution, generosity or self-protection, love or disdain. Voices ring from past teachers and critics, worried partners, and our own logic. But if we listen deeply we might hear quieter words in more resonant tones.

The spirit is prone to movement. It moves over waters to spring creation into life. It breathes into hearts and minds, bringing about change, disturbing our own waters, whispering to our hearts that there is more, that we should try, and that we are enough.

There may be times when the voice seems to fall silent, and in dark-night moments the silence can feel profound. Sometimes God calls us into deeper trust through that experience. But even in the lack of words, the divine whispers "now *you* speak love into the world," challenging us to be for others the things we hunger for in the depths of our own souls. Calling *us* to become Immanuel.

The divine whisper encourages you to seek and find, to ask and receive, to love and be loved. Try and listen for it.

You must wait and listen for the sound of the genuine that is within.
When you hear it, it will be your voice and that will be the voice of God.
Howard Thurman

Day 35: Reincarnate Here and Now

The idea that souls must be purified before uniting fully with the universal force of love crosses religions and faith traditions. Whether we're hoping to arrive in Buddhist Nirvana, Christian heaven, Hindu Moksha, or other places of post-death bliss, enlightened, cleansed states are often a requirement for entry. The process for obtaining this soul-polishing varies. Roman Catholicism describes it as purgatory, where all our imperfections are burned away, while Hinduism, Jainism, Buddhism, and Sikhism all present reincarnation as the mechanism for refinement.

Not all Christians ascribe to the view that souls need to be gussied up, believing instead that reciting the sinner's prayer or simply having faith in Jesus as Lord and savior permits immediate entry into heaven. But our faith journeys can be aided by the concept of spiritual cleansing, without needing to focus on how the whole thing works, or what it should be called.

Deconstruction offers an opportunity for entering the clean-up process actively. You may need to atone for hurt you caused others by believing what you did. Maybe you lambasted LGBTQIA+ folks on social media, or lectured a teenager when they came out. Maybe you preached hellfire and brimstone to a Sunday School class. Or maybe the wrongs you did because of your understanding of God and faith were more subtle. Regardless of what occurred—if anything—we're refined when we address our wrongdoings, seek forgiveness, work toward societal change, and attempt to undo tangible damage.

Divine love is with us as we try to get our soul polishing done regardless of what may come later. Open yourself to the burnishing which may result, and see what magic might take place through and after it.

Remember, this day will never dawn again.
Dante Alighieri

DAY 36: ASK QUESTIONS

Christians often avoid challenging questions about God, the Bible, or church by saying "God's ways are higher than our ways," or "who are we to question God?" Parents and ministry leaders often shut down our questioning, which teaches us to keep our mouths—and our minds—shut.

During deconstruction, you might fear that questions could lead to an unraveling so deep there is no return from it. If you're in that space, allow the emotion to exist until it falls away. Don't give it more energy and attention than it deserves, and don't stuff it down and pretend it's not there. Simply let the emotion exist until it doesn't anymore, and then let your inquiries flow.

The divine is not threatened by the ponderings of your brain. The author of intellect loves its use. God is not insulted when you wonder. The force of love has planted the urge to probe so we can look deeper to find them.

The first step to receiving an answer is being brave enough to ask a question. God waits for you on the other side of your wondering.

If you believe in God, whatever God you believe in, you must eventually come to the place where you understand that this God must be gracious enough for you to question your belief in this God.
David Hayward

Day 37: Invite Wonder

During a period of silence at a retreat years ago, I sat beneath a tree on the shore of a lake, thinking, praying, and watching the water. Large-grained, gritty sand collected in the tree roots, and I scooped up a handful to take a closer look. As I peered more closely, the grains which looked uniform came into focus, transforming into minute shells, shining bits of glass, and tiny polished stones, in a tumble of different shapes and sizes. The glorious variety was hidden into uniformity by the filters of perspective and distance.

In this era of fear, political tension, and endless social media outrage, it's easy to become jaded. We're constantly presented with reasons to be discouraged. The world becomes drab as we process the ongoing stress, making it hard to access joy. Assessing our view of faith and grappling with the losses which result makes it even harder.

But our lives are filled with magic and meaning, if we stop, breathe, and look more closely. The wonder of a sky turning into stripes of pink and blue at sunset, the warmth of blankets covering us on a cold night, the miraculous complexity of skin, changing texture as it performs its function of containment year after year. There is wonder to be found in simply closing our eyes and counting how many sounds we can identify, and how much life can be experienced through that focus; sounds of children playing, birds, singing, and fire trucks wailing in the distance.

It takes work to actively reject jadedness and replace it with surprise, but as we cope with the challenges of deconstruction, it's important work.

The divine is in the details. Seek them there.

> *But you don't have to be religious in order to open to wonder. You only have to reclaim a sliver of what you once knew as a child. If you remember how to wonder, then you already have what you need to learn how to love.*
> Valarie Kaur

Day 38: Resist the Urge to Reinstate Order

States of disorder feel dangerous, and the discomfort can send you rushing to replace old rules and belief parameters with something new. But disorder has a place, and a function.

Your old beliefs are like a tower of wood *Jenga* blocks. When you start pulling out timbers, the pillar eventually tumbles into disarray. Grief for the loss of structure is normal, because the creation of your faith took effort to assemble, and you've grown used to its tall orderliness. When the bland wood of *Jenga* rectangles tumbles you'll be tempted by a new set of building blocks, this time, in different shapes and hues. Yellow columns. Blue squares. Red triangles. Purple arches. Your brain might light up with possibilities and reassurance from this newer, brighter set, and you'll be tempted to assume your new creations provide the fullness of truth you've been seeking.

Childrens' building blocks are wonderful, creative things, and structural improvements over the beige uniformity of *Jenga*. But if kids cling to these simple toys, they miss out on the joys of *Lego*, complex jigsaw puzzles, and countless other tools for exploring the boundaries of their own creativity and insight.

Clinging to early replacements for your unlearned faith prevents you from seeing the wonders which lie outside it. It's fine to cherish the colorful new building blocks which emerge from your initial deconstruction, just don't let them be the final destination Hold on to what is true and beautiful, but keep your mind and heart open, and see what new fascinations God offers.

> *I don't know exactly what a prayer is.*
> *I do know how to pay attention, how to fall down*
> *into the grass, how to kneel down in the grass,*
> *how to be idle and blessed, how to stroll through the fields,*
> *which is what I have been doing all day.*
> *Tell me, what else should I have done?*
> Mary Oliver

Day 39: Be Careful with People

Dealing with people during deconstruction can be complicated. We're angry at those who've contributed to our state of mind, impatient with people who haven't joined us on the journey of unlearning, and eager to replace the spiritual leaders we've left behind. This mix of emotions can lead to all sorts of relational problems, so here are a few words of advice:

- Be selective with whom you share vulnerabilities. Deconstruction can be a tender time of examining the ways in which you were wrong, perhaps even abusively so. Companions on the journey are a wonderful thing, and the number of people deconstructing increases daily, but not everyone is capable of providing the kind of healing support many of us need as we traverse the process. Give some thought to how fragile you are and how vulnerable your progress, and select deconstruction companions based on that assessment.

- Be patient with those who aren't deconstructing. You were where they are not long ago. Permit your new-found expansion of thought to feed your compassion, wisdom, and generosity in conversation with those who remain behind.

- Anger can be easier to manage than fear but be careful with people while experiencing that emotion. Anger will pass and transform into something new, but words spoken out of vindictiveness often sow regret.

- Resist latching on to a guru as a replacement for the priest or pastor of your church, the evangelical writer or online presence you followed, or the seemingly wise family member who formed your faith. Not having spiritual leadership can feel scary, so when you need encouragement or focus for progress, consider listening to a variety of messengers rather than any single voice.

You have every reason to be upset with people who played a role in your faith life. But be careful with them, if only for your own sake.

> *It's painful when God is leading you to a place, where other people who have been important on your journey cannot follow. Don't judge them, nor judge where you've been. God was "back there" too, and still is. Don't let your heart be arrogant now. But also… don't stop walking.*
> Jonathan Martin

Day 40: Look Toward the Light

Light is a powerful thing, not only for illuminating the world around us, but for eliminating disquiet. It makes me think of a night long ago, when I wound my way through the woods toward the outhouse at my ex-husband's family cottage. The privy was set a fair distance away from the central compound, and the walk curved around and down, out of sight and away from the light of the buildings. My flashlight's beam illuminated the pine-needle-strewn path but little else. There was nothing to fear in that quiet space of looming trees. No people for miles. Bears bedded down elsewhere and uninterested in my proximity. Squirrels and chipmunks startling in their scurry but welcome company. But it was eerie, walking toward the increasing darkness. Leaving the light behind.

It was always a relief to head back afterward, knowing that in another few steps the light from the cottage would appear around a final bend.

What a difference the disposition of light makes to our feelings of safety and comfort. Even though walking in the same place, when I faced the darkness there was fear and subtle dread. When I faced the beckoning light there was expectation and hope. The actual safety of the space was exactly the same. I was no farther or closer to danger, no more or less content with the mess that was my marriage, and my being was the same facing either direction.

But the light made all the difference.

We can handle a lot of darkness in our lives as long as there are sources of light to turn to. May we all both seek it, and be it.

There is always light. If only we're brave enough to see it. If only we're brave enough to be it.
Amanda Gorman

Day 41: Laugh a Little

Research shows that shaping your face muscles into a smile makes you feel better. The physical act of smiling releases neuropeptides which help fight off stress, and laughter releases endorphins which reduce symptoms of depression.

In times of war, pandemic, and internal turmoil, small things become increasingly important. Unlearning can feel like a crisis, but the earth continues to rotate and glide around the sun, filled with pleasures and joys even when things are at their worst. Once you get over the initial gulps of deconstruction sorrow and recognize you aren't drowning, seek the humor in situations related to the process.

Laugh at your hubris.

Laugh at the idea of a God who can be fully known or contained by a book.

Laugh at the knowledge that where you are now is not where you'll be in a year, or in a decade.

Laugh at the silly things your pets, friends, or co-workers do.

Search out humor.

It doesn't matter if you manufacture ways of generating smiles and laughter rather than experiencing them organically. The physical actions make a difference. So watch funny movies, listen to comedians, and hang out with people who make you giggle. Let laughter do the work of healing.

> *Laugh till you weep. Weep till there's nothing left but to laugh at your weeping. In the end it's all one.*
> Frederick Buechner

Day 42: Increase Your Awareness of God in All Things

The "philosophy of consciousness" explores the idea that some form of cognizance exists at every level of existence. Plants have an awareness of the sun, turning their faces toward it as their pots are rotated on a kitchen window. The roots of trees transmit chemical messages to their neighbors signaling when to conserve resources. Microorganisms "know" they need to waggle cilia or stretch a pseudopod to move somewhere other than the place they presently float. Hydrogen and oxygen atoms become aware of each other and merge to form the water protozoa float in. Even within those atoms, protons and neutrons huddle so attractively that electrons can't help but circle.

We humans view ourselves as the height of consciousness with our ability to think, judge, and act. But in light of divine omniscience, our awareness is as self-focused and limited as an amoeba surrounding and dissolving its prey.

God adored their creation from the moment the Big Bang exploded the energy which transformed into stars and planets and you and I. They are saturated in every mote of dust miraculously sparkling as it drifts in the shaft of sunlight falling through the door of your bedroom, every black hole pulling in time, space, and light with astounding gravity, and every tyrannical politician and self-donating fighter for justice. God's consciousness is so deep it merges into mutual experience with each bit of matter, participating in the interconnection of the rot of death, the planting of life, and the multitude of things which happen far outside our own cognition.

Each of these connections is imbued with divinity. God is in everything and aware of everything, and each thing carries within it the potential to be aware of each other thing.

Hebrew and Christian scripture tells us to be holy because God is holy. But the holiness of God has nothing to do with biblical rules and regulations, and everything to do with the love which saturates all of creation.

Maybe the goal of faith isn't to memorize Bible passages and adhere to a particular set of rules as set down in scripture. Maybe the goal is to have an ever-expanding awareness of the glowing presence of the divine in and through all things; an ongoing expansion of consciousness.

It's okay to unfurl your grip on the Bible, church, and Christianity as you've understood it, and shift toward raising and expanding your awareness of God in all things.

Be holy as God is holy.

This beloved soul was preciously knitted to God in its making, by a knot so subtle and so mighty that it is oned in God. In this oneing, it is made endlessly holy. Furthermore, God wants us to know that all the souls which will be saved in heaven without end are knit in this knot, and oned in this oneing, and made holy in this holiness.
Lady Julian of Norwich

Day 43: Keep Going

As your deconstruction process unfolds, you might feel like a deer in the headlights; stunned, stuck, and unable to move out of fear something really horrendous could result. You might be wrapped in a cloak of ennui, unable to move or even care. You might even experience a desire to go backward, back to where things felt safe and you knew the boundaries and textures of the world.

But it's not possible to go back. You have only two choices: to stay where and who you are, right now, or to move forward into the new.

The extremity of tension doesn't last forever. Things continue to shift and your views and fears will shift along with them. Allow yourself to be carried for a bit, floating in the movement of what is happening rather than fighting the tide. The water is bigger and more powerful than you are, and submitting to where it wants to carry you is easier and more productive than thrashing in protest, demanding to remain in your current position.

Anger might try to drag you down. Don't let it.

Fear might try to swamp you. Don't give in to it.

Fatigue might hit. Rest for a bit, but don't sleep forever.

Allow the change to happen. Push through the discomfort, so you can be carried ashore. There will be much to explore in this new place; things which will bring joy and new questions, an expanse of wonder opening up in wave after wave.

But you have to be brave.

Keep going.

And thus a soul is greatly impeded from reaching this high estate of union with God, when it clings to any understanding or feeling or imagination or appearance or will or manner of its own ... For as we say, the goal which it seeks lies beyond all this, yea, even beyond the highest thing that can be known or experienced, and thus a soul must pass beyond everything to unknowing.
St. John of the Cross

Conclusion

We've finished our time together, but the work isn't done. I'm still on the path and probably always will be. There'll be more dark nights for my spirit, more moments of intense certainty, and more phases in which I feel like Paul on the road to Damascus; rendered blind by the light, fumbling and mourning my losses before resigning myself to the reality of the ways I've been wrong and the invitation to open my mind to the glory of a reality that is impossibly grand.

As you continue moving through deconstruction, I pray you'll feel truth shining, calling, drawing you near, and that the light will give you comfort and peace in times of uncertainty.

God is always coming out of a formless void into revelation. The space of emptiness is rich with anticipation, and fertile with promise.

May we always be receptive to the potential of more.

www.ingramcontent.com/pod-product-compliance
Lightning Source LLC
Chambersburg PA
CBHW060216050426
42446CB00013B/3085